# AI Automation Agency Blueprint: A Comprehensive Guide to Building a Profitable Business with Zapier

# Table of Contents

  - Identifying Your Niche

  - Crafting a Solid Business Plan

## 5. Setting Up Your AI Automation Agency

  - Legal Considerations and Structure

  - Building Your Team

  - Office Setup and Equipment Needs

## 6. Developing AI Automation Solutions with Zapier

  - Working with Clients: Needs Assessment and Solution Design

  - Building and Testing AI Automation Solutions using Zapier

  - Case Studies of Successful Implementations

## 7. Marketing Your AI Automation Agency

  - Branding and Positioning Your Agency

  - Online and Offline Marketing Strategies

  - Building Strategic Partnerships

## 12. Conclusion

- Key Takeaways

- Your Next Steps to AI Automation Success

# Chapter 1: Introduction

## The Rise of AI and Automation

Artificial intelligence and automation have revolutionized the world in ways that were unimaginable just a few decades ago. Advances in machine learning and cognitive computing have given birth to systems that can understand, learn, predict, and react—functioning in ways similar to the human brain.

AI is reshaping industries, creating new business models, and opening up a myriad of opportunities for entrepreneurs. One such opportunity lies in process automation, where AI systems can take over routine, mundane tasks, thereby improving efficiency, reducing errors, and freeing up human workers to focus on more strategic tasks.

Automation, fueled by AI, has the potential to deliver substantial economic benefits. According to McKinsey, it could raise global productivity by as much as 1.4% annually. From customer service chatbots to automated marketing campaigns and smart CRM systems, businesses are finding new ways to leverage AI and automation.

In a recent survey by Salesforce, 51% of marketers are already using AI, and more than a quarter plan to start within the next two years. In another survey by Deloitte, 57% of businesses said that automation technologies are either transforming or contributing significantly to their organizations.

**Why Start an AI Automation Agency?**

Starting an AI automation agency offers the opportunity to ride this wave of technological advancement. Businesses of all sizes, across industries, are recognizing the value of automation but often lack the expertise to implement it effectively. They need partners who can help them navigate this new landscape, identify opportunities for automation, and implement solutions that can drive productivity and performance.

As the owner of an AI automation agency, you could be that partner. You could help businesses leverage the power of AI to automate their processes, improve customer experiences, and unlock new levels of efficiency.

Apart from the vast market potential, starting an AI automation agency can be a highly rewarding venture, both intellectually and financially. You'll be at the forefront of AI development, working with exciting technologies, solving complex problems, and seeing the tangible impact of your work as businesses transform and thrive thanks to the solutions you provide.

**Introduction to Zapier**

One of the tools that make this venture possible, even for those without a deep background in AI or coding, is Zapier. Zapier is an online automation tool that connects your favorite apps, allowing you to automate repetitive tasks without coding or relying on developers to build the integration.

With its easy-to-use interface, Zapier allows you to set up automated workflows, known as 'Zaps'. A 'Zap' consists of a 'trigger' and one or more 'actions'. The 'trigger' is the event in the source app that starts the Zap. Once you set up a Zap, Zapier will monitor the trigger app for that event.

Zapier supports over 2,000 apps, including common business tools like Gmail, Slack, Mailchimp, Google Sheets, Salesforce, and many more. The possibilities for automation with Zapier are virtually endless, from simple tasks like transferring email attachments to Dropbox to more complex workflows involving multiple apps and conditions.

This book is your comprehensive guide to starting and scaling an AI automation agency, with Zapier as your primary tool. From understanding AI and automation concepts to setting up your agency, developing solutions, and acquiring clients, we will walk through each step of the journey. The future is here, and it's automated. Let's get started.

**Chapter 2: Understanding Artificial Intelligence and Automation**

## Basics of AI and Machine Learning

Artificial Intelligence (AI) is a branch of computer science that aims to imbue software with the ability to analyze its environment using either predetermined rules and search algorithms, or pattern recognizing machine learning models, and make decisions that maximize its chance of achieving its goals.

The concept of AI has been around since the 1950s, but recent developments in technology and data availability have significantly accelerated progress in this field. Today, AI is becoming an integral part of our daily lives, from voice assistants like Alexa and Siri to recommendation engines on Netflix or Amazon.

Machine Learning (ML), a subset of AI, involves the practice of using algorithms to parse data, learn from it, and then make a prediction or decision about something in the world. Instead of hand-coding software routines with specific instructions to accomplish a particular task, the machine is trained using large amounts of data and algorithms to learn how to perform the task.

Machine learning models are often categorized as supervised or unsupervised. Supervised machine learning models are trained on labeled data. For example, a model might be trained to recognize images of cars by being shown thousands of labeled images of cars. On the other hand, unsupervised machine learning models are trained on unlabeled data and must find patterns in the data on their own.

## Role of AI in Automation

The goal of automation is to minimize human intervention and make processes more efficient, accurate, and reliable. AI plays a crucial role in achieving this goal by adding an element of intelligence to automation. This fusion is often referred to as intelligent automation.

AI-powered automation can be seen in various applications across industries. In customer service, AI chatbots are being used to automate responses to common queries, thereby reducing response times and freeing up human agents to handle more complex queries. In manufacturing, AI-powered robots are being used to automate tasks that were traditionally performed by humans.

In marketing, AI is used to automate tasks such as content creation, personalized advertising, and customer segmentation. In healthcare, AI is automating tasks ranging from appointment scheduling to more complex ones like diagnosing diseases from medical images.

AI not only automates tasks but also learns from the data it processes, thereby improving its performance over time. For example, an AI chatbot learns from each interaction it has with users and becomes better at understanding and responding to queries.

**How Zapier Facilitates Automation**

Zapier is a cloud-based service that allows end users to integrate the web applications they use. Although this is a form of automation, it is not inherently an AI solution. However, Zapier provides the scaffolding on which an AI-powered automation system can be built.

Zapier connects different applications and allows for data flow between them, creating automated workflows called Zaps. For instance, you can create a Zap that saves your Gmail attachments to Dropbox and alerts you in Slack about the new Dropbox file.

Zapier makes automation accessible to non-developers, democratizing a capability that was once reserved for those with advanced technical skills. You can choose from thousands of pre-made workflows, or you can create your own with an easy, step-by-step process.

Zapier has a vast library of over 2000 apps that it can connect, including all the most commonly used online apps. When it comes to an AI Automation Agency, Zapier allows the development and deployment of automated processes that your clients can use. Whether it's automating social media posts, tracking metrics, or managing customer relationships, Zapier can facilitate it all.

Through Zapier, businesses can set up complex, AI-powered automation systems without needing a vast amount of technical expertise. By connecting AI tools, like Dialogflow or Watson, with Zapier, businesses can create powerful automation workflows that leverage the best of AI.

In the following chapters, we will explore how you can harness the power of Zapier to build a profitable AI Automation Agency. We will look at the specific steps involved in setting up your agency, defining your services, marketing your business, and ensuring that your clients get the best results from their investment in AI and automation.

## Chapter 3: Exploring Zapier's Capabilities

### Overview of Zapier's Features

Zapier's strength lies in its simplicity and flexibility. With Zapier, you can automate tasks between different web applications without needing to write any code. Here are some key features of Zapier:

**1. Wide Range of Apps:** Zapier supports over 2,000 web apps, including most popular apps like Gmail, Slack, Google Sheets, Trello, and more.

**2. Zaps:** The basic building block of Zapier is a 'Zap', which is an automated workflow that connects your apps and services together. A Zap consists of a 'trigger' and one or more 'actions'. The trigger is the event in the source app that starts the Zap. Once you set up a Zap, Zapier will monitor the source app for that event. When the event happens, Zapier automatically completes the action(s) in other app(s) that you've defined.

**3. Multi-Step Zaps:** While a basic Zap consists of one trigger and one action, a Multi-Step Zap has one trigger and two or more actions. This allows you to build more complex workflows and automate multiple tasks at once.

**4. Filters:** Filters allow you to control when your Zap runs. By setting up a filter, you can specify certain conditions for the trigger event, and the Zap will only run when those conditions are met.

**5. Paths:** Paths are like conditional logic for your Zaps. With paths, your Zap will follow different routes based on the characteristics of your trigger event. This allows you to build more complex, logic-based workflows.

Creating your first Zap might seem a bit intimidating at first, but Zapier's user-friendly interface makes it a straightforward process. To illustrate, let's walk through an example of a common business use case: automatically saving email attachments to Google Drive and notifying the team on Slack.

## Use Case: Automatically Save Email Attachments to Google Drive and Notify Team on Slack

### Step 1: Choose your trigger app

Your trigger app is where your Zap begins. In this case, our trigger app will be Gmail, as we want the Zap to start when we receive an email with an attachment.

### Step 2: Select the trigger event

Each app has a list of possible trigger events. For Gmail, we have several options, including 'New Email', 'New Thread', 'New Starred Email', etc. In this scenario, we will choose 'New Attachment in Email' as our trigger event.

## Step 3: Choose your action app

Next, we need to specify what should happen when the trigger event occurs. We want to save the attachment to Google Drive, so we will choose Google Drive as our first action app.

## Step 4: Select the action event

Just like trigger events, each app also has several possible action events. For Google Drive, these include 'Upload File', 'Create Folder', 'Find File', etc. We will choose 'Upload File' as our action event.

## Step 5: Set up your action

Setting up your action requires you to specify certain details related to the action event. In this case, we'll need to specify which file (the email attachment) to upload and where to save it in Google Drive.

**Step 6: Add another action**

Now, we want to notify the team on Slack that a new file has been added to Google Drive. For that, we add another action and choose Slack as our second action app.

**Step 7: Select the action event for Slack**

We need to select 'Send Channel Message' as the action event, as we want to notify the entire team.

**Step 8: Set up your action for Slack**

We then set up the message we want to send, specifying the channel and the message content (e.g., "A new file has been added to Google Drive").

**Step 9: Turn on your Zap**

The final step is to turn on your Zap. Once you've done that, Zapier will monitor your Gmail for new attachments, automatically upload any attachments to Google Drive, and notify your team on Slack each time a new file is added.

By automating this workflow, businesses can save valuable time, reduce the chance of error, and ensure timely notifications. With Zapier, countless such workflows can be automated, making life easier and boosting productivity. Now imagine the potential when you, as an AI Automation Agency, offer to build such automations tailored to specific business needs.

## Use Case: Automatically Add New HubSpot Contacts to Google Sheets

Many businesses use a CRM like HubSpot to manage their customer relationships, and Google Sheets to manage internal processes or reporting. A common need is to have new contacts from HubSpot automatically added to a Google Sheets spreadsheet.

### Step 1: Choose your trigger app

In this case, our trigger app will be HubSpot because we want the Zap to start when a new contact is added to our HubSpot CRM.

### Step 2: Select the trigger event

For HubSpot, we have several options including 'New Contact', 'New Company', 'New Deal', etc. In this scenario, we choose 'New Contact' as our trigger event.

## Step 3: Choose your action app

Next, we decide what should happen when the trigger event occurs. We want to add the contact information to a Google Sheets spreadsheet, so Google Sheets will be our action app.

## Step 4: Select the action event

For Google Sheets, we have several options including 'Create Spreadsheet Row', 'Update Spreadsheet Row', 'Find Spreadsheet Row', etc. We will select 'Create Spreadsheet Row' as our action event.

## Step 5: Set up your action

Setting up your action requires specifying certain details related to the action event. We'll need to specify which spreadsheet and which worksheet within that spreadsheet to add the new contact information to. We'll also need to map the contact information fields from HubSpot (like first name, last name, email, etc.) to the columns in our Google Sheets worksheet.

**Step 6: Turn on your Zap**

The final step is to turn on your Zap. Once it's on, Zapier will monitor your HubSpot for new contacts and automatically add them to your Google Sheets spreadsheet.

With this automation, businesses can ensure that their CRM and spreadsheets are always in sync without needing any manual intervention. This not only saves time but also ensures data accuracy and timely updates.

The opportunity as an AI Automation Agency here is to help businesses identify such automation opportunities and then configure and manage them using Zapier. You can provide valuable services to businesses by understanding their processes and recommending efficient automation strategies.

**Advanced Zapier Concepts: Multi-Step Zaps, Paths, and Filters**

Zapier's advanced features allow you to build more complex workflows. Here's a brief overview:

**Multi-Step Zaps:** With Multi-Step Zaps, you can chain together several actions after your trigger event. For example, when a new email arrives (trigger), you can save the attachment to Dropbox (action 1), add a new row in Google

Sheets (action 2), and send a notification on Slack (action 3), all in one go.

**Paths:** Paths allow your Zap to take different routes based on the details of the trigger event. For instance, if an email comes from a certain address (trigger), you can set up different paths to handle it differently based on the subject line.

**Filters:** Filters allow you to set up conditions that the trigger event must meet for the Zap to run. For instance, if you want to automate responding to emails, but only if the email comes from a particular client, you can set this up using a filter.

In the next chapters, we will delve deeper into these concepts, showing you how to leverage them to build effective, customized automation workflows for your clients. By mastering these, you will be well on your way to building a successful AI Automation Agency.

# Chapter 4: Market Research and Business Planning

In this chapter, we will delve into the foundational steps you need to take before setting up your AI Automation Agency. We will begin by understanding the landscape of AI automation, identifying your niche, and crafting a robust business plan.

## Understanding the AI Automation Landscape

Artificial Intelligence (AI) and automation are revolutionizing the way businesses operate. They enable enterprises to automate routine tasks, thus freeing up human resources to focus on more strategic initiatives. Here's what the AI automation landscape looks like:

**1. Industry Adoption:** AI automation is being adopted across a wide array of sectors, including manufacturing, healthcare, finance, retail, and more. Each sector presents its own unique challenges and opportunities.

**2. Competition:** There are several players in the AI automation space, from tech giants like IBM and Google to numerous start-ups. Understanding the competitive landscape can help you differentiate your services and find your unique selling proposition (USP).

**3. Regulations:** Depending on your geographic location and target industries, there may be specific regulations around data privacy and AI usage that you need to be aware of.

**4. Technologies:** Familiarize yourself with the latest AI and automation technologies, including machine learning algorithms, robotic process automation (RPA) tools, and platforms like Zapier. Keeping up-to-date with technology trends will allow you to provide the most advanced and efficient solutions to your clients.

## Identifying Your Niche

Once you have a good understanding of the landscape, it's time to find your niche. Your niche will define who your target clients are and what specific services you offer. Here are a few steps to identify your niche:

**1. Identify Market Needs:** Start by identifying the needs and pain points in the market that you can address. These could be specific processes that businesses struggle to automate, or certain sectors that are lagging in AI adoption.

**2. Leverage Your Strengths:** What are you particularly good at? What is your expertise? Leverage these strengths to define your niche. For example, if you have experience in the healthcare industry, you could focus on providing AI automation services for healthcare providers.

**3. Consider Your Interests:** Doing what you love can significantly contribute to your success. Consider your interests when choosing your niche.

## Crafting a Solid Business Plan

Once you've defined your niche, it's time to craft a solid business plan. Your business plan should detail your business model, marketing strategy, financial plan, and operational plan. Here are the key elements:

**1. Executive Summary:** This is an overview of your business and your plans. It should summarize your business, the problem you're solving, your solution, target market, and financial projections.

**2. Company Description:** This section should provide detailed information about your company and what you do. It should outline your business structure, ownership, types of services you offer, and the needs of your clients that you aim to meet.

**3. Market Analysis:** In this section, you should analyze your industry, market, and competition. Use your research on the AI automation landscape and your niche to guide this analysis.

**4. Organization and Management:** This section should describe your company's organizational structure and the team managing your business. Include an organizational chart if applicable.

**5. Services:** Describe in detail the AI automation services you're offering. Highlight the benefits your services provide and how they differentiate from the competition.

**6. Marketing and Sales Strategy:** Outline your marketing and sales strategy. This should include your strategies for lead generation, conversion, and customer retention.

**7. Financial Projections:** Provide an overview of your financial projections. Include forecasted income statements, balance sheets, and cash flow statements for the next five years.

**8. Funding Request (If applicable):** If you're seeking funding, outline your funding request. Explain how the funds will be used and the type of return investors can expect.

Building a successful AI Automation Agency begins with a deep understanding of the market, a clearly defined niche, and a solid business plan.

This foundation will guide your decisions and strategies as you navigate your entrepreneurial journey in the exciting world of AI automation.

## Chapter 5: Setting Up Your AI Automation Agency

Starting your AI Automation Agency requires careful planning and consideration. In this chapter, we will discuss the legal considerations, team building, and setting up the necessary infrastructure.

### Legal Considerations and Structure

Determining the legal structure of your business is one of the first things you should do. The structure you choose will affect your business registration requirements, the amount of taxes you'll need to pay, and your personal liability. Here are the most common types:

**1. Sole Proprietorship:** This is the simplest type, suitable for individuals who own their businesses entirely. Remember, the owner is personally responsible for all the company's debts.

**2. Partnership:** If you plan on having a business partner, a partnership might be the appropriate choice. Partnerships can be either general or limited.

**3. Corporation:** A corporation is a separate entity from its owners, providing personal liability protection. It requires more extensive record-keeping and reporting.

**4. Limited Liability Company (LLC):** An LLC offers liability protection like a corporation, but with simpler tax and administrative requirements.

You also need to consider legal aspects like business licenses and permits, intellectual property protection, and data privacy regulations. Consulting with a business attorney can provide insights tailored to your specific circumstances.

**Building Your Team**

Building a talented and motivated team is critical for the success of your AI Automation Agency. Here are the roles you should consider:

**1. AI Specialists:** These are the people who will understand the ins and outs of AI, machine learning, and automation. They will be responsible for creating and maintaining the AI models that drive your solutions.

**2. Zapier Experts:** You'll need team members proficient in using Zapier to connect various applications and automate tasks based on the AI models.

**3. Sales and Marketing:** A sales and marketing team will help promote your services, secure clients, and build relationships.

**4. Customer Support:** Excellent customer support can set your agency apart. This team will provide assistance to clients and help troubleshoot any issues they encounter.

**5. Administrative Staff:** This includes roles like HR, finance, and general administration to ensure smooth business operations.

## Office Setup and Equipment Needs

Your office setup will depend on your team size and the way you choose to operate – remote, in-office, or a hybrid model. Here are the key considerations:

**1. Physical Office:** If you plan to operate from an office, you'll need to consider the location, size, layout, and utilities. Ensure there's enough space for your team to work comfortably and have access to necessary facilities.

**2. Remote Setup:** If your team will work remotely, invest in good collaboration tools to ensure seamless communication. Tools like Slack for communication, Trello for project management, and Google Suite for document sharing can be very effective.

**3. Equipment:** Regardless of where your team works, they'll need the right equipment. This usually includes computers with adequate processing power, monitors, keyboards, mice, and ergonomic chairs.

**4. Software:** Your team will require various software tools to carry out their tasks. This may include AI and machine learning tools, cloud services, Zapier, and CRM software.

Setting up your AI Automation Agency is a significant step that will lay the foundation for your operations. Proper legal structure, an effective team, and a conducive work environment will go a long way towards ensuring the success of your agency. Remember, it's all about creating an environment that fosters innovation, collaboration, and customer-centricity.

## Chapter 6: Developing AI Automation Solutions with Zapier

One of the main functions of your AI Automation Agency will be to develop solutions that address your clients' needs. In this chapter, we delve into the process of working with clients, from needs assessment to solution design and implementation, using Zapier as our tool of choice.

**Working with Clients: Needs Assessment and Solution Design**

Before you can build an AI automation solution, you must understand the client's needs. This process involves several steps:

**1. Initial Meeting:** Conduct an initial meeting with your client to discuss their challenges, goals, and vision for automation.

**2. Needs Assessment:** Review their existing systems and processes in detail to identify areas that could benefit from automation.

**3. Solution Design:** Design an automation solution that aligns with the client's needs and objectives. This should include a detailed description of the workflows to be automated, the apps to be integrated, and the expected outcomes.

**4. Proposal:** Present your solution to the client, including an overview of the project, timelines, costs, and expected benefits.

Remember, communication is key during this process. Regularly engage with your client to ensure that your proposed solution aligns with their needs and expectations.

**Building and Testing AI Automation Solutions using Zapier**

Once the client approves the solution design, the next step is to build it using Zapier. This involves several steps:

**1. Building the Workflow:** Use Zapier to create the necessary 'Zaps' that automate the client's workflows. This will involve selecting the appropriate trigger and action apps, defining the trigger and action events, and setting up the action details.

**2. Testing:** Thorough testing is crucial to ensure that your automation solution works as expected. Test each Zap in different scenarios to identify and correct any issues.

**3. Client Review:** Once testing is complete, review the solution with your client. Make any necessary adjustments based on their feedback.

**4. Deployment:** After the client approves the solution, deploy it in their live environment.

**5. Monitoring and Optimization:** Monitor the solution's performance over time and make adjustments as needed to optimize its effectiveness.

## Case Studies of Successful Implementations

To illustrate the potential of AI automation with Zapier, let's consider a couple of case studies.

**1. Marketing Agency:** A marketing agency used Zapier to automate their social media posting. They created a Zap that triggers whenever a new blog post is published on their website. The Zap then creates and publishes social media posts on various platforms, saving the agency hours of manual work each week.

**2. E-commerce Company:** An e-commerce company used Zapier to automate their customer service. They created a Zap that triggers whenever a customer leaves a negative review. The Zap then sends an email to the customer service team, who can promptly address the customer's concerns.

These case studies illustrate how businesses can use Zapier to automate tasks, improve efficiency, and enhance their services. As an AI Automation Agency, your role is to create such transformative solutions for your clients.

Building effective AI automation solutions with Zapier involves understanding your client's needs, designing and implementing solutions, and continuously monitoring and optimizing them. By doing this effectively, you can help your clients transform their operations and drive their success.

# Chapter 7: Marketing Your AI Automation Agency

Establishing your agency is just the first step. The real challenge lies in making your mark in the industry, attracting the right clients, and fostering long-term partnerships. This chapter will guide you through various aspects of marketing, from branding your agency to exploring online and offline strategies, and building strategic partnerships.

## Branding and Positioning Your Agency

The process of branding starts with understanding your unique selling proposition (USP) - what sets you apart from other AI automation agencies. Your USP is the core of your brand and should be reflected in all your marketing materials.

Here are the steps to build your brand:

**1. Define Your Brand:** What does your agency represent? How are you different? Define your mission, vision, and values.

**2. Identify Your Target Audience:** Who can benefit the most from your services? Define your ideal client. This could be a small business owner, an operations manager in a large corporation, or an IT manager, among others.

**3. Design Your Brand Elements:** This includes your logo, color palette, fonts, and other visual elements that represent your agency. These elements should resonate with your target audience and convey your brand's personality.

**4. Craft Your Brand Message:** This is a clear and concise statement that communicates what you do, who you do it for, and why you're different.

**5. Position Your Brand:** Position your brand in a way that distinguishes you from your competitors. This can be based on factors like quality, expertise, customer service, or price.

## Online and Offline Marketing Strategies

Once you've built your brand, it's time to market your agency. Let's explore some strategies:

### Online Strategies

**1. Website:** Create a professional website that showcases your services, case studies, testimonials, and blog posts. Optimize it for SEO to make it easier for potential clients to find you.

**2. Social Media:** Leverage platforms like LinkedIn, Twitter, and Facebook to share valuable content, engage with your audience, and promote your services.

**3. Email Marketing:** Build an email list and regularly send out newsletters or promotional materials. This can help you stay top of mind with your audience.

**4. Content Marketing:** Regularly publish blog posts, ebooks, webinars, or videos that provide value to your audience. This can help establish your agency as an authority in AI automation.

**5. Paid Advertising:** Consider running paid ads on platforms like Google Ads or LinkedIn to reach a larger audience.

**Offline Strategies**

1. **Networking Events:** Attend industry events, conferences, or meetups to connect with potential clients and partners.

2. **Speaking Engagements:** Offer to speak at events or workshops. This can help position you as an expert and attract potential clients.

3. **Direct Mail:** Although it's a more traditional method, direct mail can still be effective, especially for local businesses.

4. **Press Releases:** Use press releases to announce major milestones or successes of your agency. This can help generate media coverage and increase your visibility.

## Building Strategic Partnerships

Partnerships can help you reach a wider audience, enhance your offerings, and grow your business. Here are some types of partnerships you could consider:

**1. Technology Partners:** Partner with technology providers like Zapier or other AI platforms. This could give you access to resources, training, or support that could benefit your clients.

**2. Agency Partners:** Partner with other agencies that offer complementary services. You could refer clients to each other or offer bundled services.

**3. Client Partners:** Foster strong relationships with your clients. They can become advocates for your agency, referring you to other potential clients.

Marketing your AI Automation Agency requires a comprehensive approach that combines branding, a variety of online and offline strategies, and strategic partnerships. Remember, marketing is a continuous process, so always track your efforts, analyze the results, and adjust your strategies as needed.

## Chapter 8: Sales and Client Acquisition

Establishing a successful client base is integral to your AI automation agency's growth and profitability. This chapter will delve into the intricacies of prospecting and lead generation, managing sales conversations, closing deals, and aligning expectations with clients.

### Prospecting and Lead Generation

Prospecting is the process of identifying potential clients who would benefit from your services. Various strategies can help you generate leads:

**1. Content Marketing:** Consistently producing relevant, high-quality content can draw potential clients to your website. For example, you might write a blog post on how automating social media posting with Zapier can save time and increase efficiency for businesses.

**2. SEO:** Optimizing your website for search engines can improve visibility and attract more potential clients. Suppose you've written a blog post about the benefits of Zapier. To increase your chances of appearing in search results, you might focus on keywords such as "benefits of Zapier," "Zapier for business," or "how to automate with Zapier."

**3. Social Media:** Engaging on social media platforms can help you foster relationships with potential clients. For example, you could host a live Q&A session on LinkedIn where you answer questions about AI automation.

**4. Email Marketing:** Collecting emails and sending out regular updates or insights can help you stay top of mind for potential clients. An email series showcasing various automation strategies for different industries could provide valuable insights to potential clients and showcase your expertise.

## Sales Conversations and Closing Deals

Once you've identified potential leads, it's crucial to turn them into clients by:

**1. Understanding Needs:** In your initial conversations, your goal should be to understand your client's needs, challenges, and goals. For instance, a client might need a solution that automates their customer support ticketing process.

**2. Present Your Solution:** After understanding their needs, present your solution tailored to their specific situation. Illustrate how automation can streamline their customer support process, reduce response times, and improve customer satisfaction.

**3. Handle Objections:** If the client has reservations, address these concerns head-on. If they're worried about the transition process, assure them of your support during the onboarding phase and the adaptability of AI automation solutions.

**4. Close the Deal:** Once you've responded to their concerns, ask for their business. Be upfront about your pricing, the expected timeline, and contract terms.

### Onboarding Clients and Managing Expectations

After securing the contract, it's time to onboard the client and set the groundwork for a productive relationship:

**1. Onboarding Process:** Outline your onboarding process. This could involve an initial kickoff meeting, introducing them to your project management tools, and gathering necessary data.

**2. Scope of Work:** Clearly articulate the scope of your work, including the services you'll offer, the project timeline, deliverables, and any underlying assumptions. This should be encapsulated in a formal contract.

**3. Communication and Reporting:** Establish clear communication lines and reporting schedules. Transparency is vital in building trust and ensuring that the client is always aware of the project status.

By using these strategies and tailoring them to your unique situation, you can create a robust client base and lay the foundation for a thriving AI automation agency.

**Chapter 9: Project Management and Delivering Value**

Project management is an essential component of running a successful AI automation agency. It's not just about delivering solutions on time but also ensuring that these solutions provide value to your clients. In this chapter, we'll discuss strategies for organizing and managing AI projects, ensuring quality and client satisfaction, and conducting post-project analysis for continuous learning and improvement.

## Organizing and Managing AI Projects

Effective project management starts with clear planning and organization. Here's a roadmap to help you manage your AI projects effectively:

**1. Project Initiation:** The first step is defining the project's scope, objectives, and deliverables. For example, if you're working on a project to automate a client's email marketing campaign using Zapier, your objectives could be to improve open rates and click-through rates, and your deliverables might include the Zapier automation setup and a comprehensive report of the results.

**2. Project Planning:** Next, create a detailed project plan. Outline the tasks required, assign responsibilities, set deadlines, and determine the resources needed. Using a project management tool, like Asana or Trello, can help you keep track of these elements.

**3. Project Execution:** With a plan in place, it's time to execute. Implement the automation solution, regularly updating your client and your team about the project's progress.

**4. Project Closure:** Once the solution is live, ensure everything is working as expected. Provide the necessary documentation and training to your client so they can manage the solution effectively.

## Ensuring Quality and Client Satisfaction

The key to a successful project isn't just delivering on time, but also ensuring high quality and client satisfaction:

**1. Quality Assurance:** Regular testing is crucial to detect and correct issues before the solution is delivered. For the email marketing automation project, you might run tests to ensure that the emails are being sent at the right time, to the right audience, and with the correct content.

**2. Feedback Loops:** Regular check-ins with your clients not only keep them updated, but also allow you to gather feedback and make necessary adjustments. This helps ensure the solution meets the client's expectations.

**3. Client Training:** Once the solution is ready, provide comprehensive training to your clients. This empowers them to effectively use the solution and increases their satisfaction.

## Post-Project Analysis and Learning

After the project is completed, it's important to conduct a post-project analysis:

**1. Performance Analysis:** Review the project's outcomes against the initial objectives. Did the automated email campaign increase open rates and click-through rates? Were there any unexpected results?

**2. Feedback Gathering:** Ask your client for feedback. Were they satisfied with the process and the outcomes? What could be improved?

**3. Lessons Learned:** Identify what went well and what didn't. For instance, if the testing phase revealed that the automation was not triggering correctly, how can you improve your testing process for future projects?

By applying these principles of project management, your AI automation agency can deliver valuable, high-quality solutions that satisfy clients and lead to successful, long-term relationships.

# Chapter 10: Scaling Your AI Automation Agency

Scaling your AI Automation Agency involves more than just growing your client base or hiring more employees. It requires a comprehensive understanding of business growth, efficient talent management, and the building of systems designed to facilitate and accommodate expansion. In this chapter, we'll explore how you can effectively scale your AI Automation agency.

## Understanding and Managing Business Growth

Business growth can be both exciting and challenging. Here are some strategies to manage growth effectively:

**1. Monitor Key Metrics:** Track metrics such as revenue, profitability, client acquisition, client retention, and project success rates. These metrics provide insights into your agency's performance and growth trajectory. For instance, if you see a consistent increase in client retention, it might be a good sign that your agency is ready for scaling.

**2. Cash Flow Management:** As your business grows, so will your expenses. Effective cash flow management is crucial to ensure you can meet your financial obligations while investing in growth. This might involve renegotiating terms with suppliers, ensuring timely payments from clients, or even securing additional funding.

**3. Strategic Planning:** Create a growth plan that outlines your business objectives, strategies to achieve them, and metrics to measure progress.

For example, if your objective is to double your client base in the next two years, your strategies might include investing in marketing, expanding your services, and entering new markets.

## Hiring and Talent Management

People are your most important resource in an AI automation agency. Here's how you can effectively manage talent as you scale:

**1. Hiring Strategically:** As your agency grows, you will need to expand your team. Rather than hiring reactively, plan your hiring strategically. For instance, if you're planning to offer new services like data analytics, you might need to hire data scientists.

**2. Developing Talent:** Invest in training and development to help your team acquire new skills and improve their performance. This can help you deliver better services and improve client satisfaction.

**3. Cultivating a Positive Culture:** As you add more people to your team, maintaining a positive and collaborative culture is crucial. This can help you retain talent and ensure your team remains motivated and productive.

**Building Systems for Scale**

Scaling your agency also requires building systems and processes that can handle increased workloads and complexity:

**1. Automation:** Automate repetitive tasks wherever possible. For instance, you could use Zapier to automate your client onboarding process, such as sending welcome emails or setting up initial meetings.

**2. Project Management Systems:** As you handle more projects, a robust project management system becomes crucial. Tools like Asana or Trello can help you track project progress, assign tasks, and manage deadlines.

**3. Client Relationship Management (CRM) Systems:** A CRM system can help you manage growing client relationships effectively. It can track client information, communication history, and project details, helping you provide personalized and efficient service.

By understanding and managing business growth, investing in people, and building robust systems, you can successfully scale your AI Automation agency, leading to increased revenue, a larger client base, and a more resilient business.

**Chapter 11: Navigating Future Trends**

The world of AI and automation is ever-evolving, and the pace of change is rapid. As you grow your AI automation agency, staying abreast of these changes is essential to maintain a competitive edge and continuously deliver value to your clients. In this chapter, we'll explore how you can navigate future trends, adapt to market changes, and stay ahead in the industry.

**Keeping Up with AI and Automation Trends**

Staying up-to-date with trends in AI and automation can help you identify opportunities for your agency and ensure your services remain relevant and valuable to your clients. Here are some strategies:

**1. Continuous Learning:** Regularly read industry publications, follow influential thought leaders on social media, and attend webinars, conferences, and workshops. These resources can provide insights into the latest advancements in AI and automation.

**2. Networking:** Build relationships with other professionals in your industry. Joining professional networks and communities can provide opportunities for collaboration, learning, and sharing of ideas.

**3. Client Feedback:** Your clients can be a valuable source of insights about industry trends. Regularly ask for their feedback and understand their evolving needs and challenges.

Let's take an example of an AI trend - the rise of AI ethics. With growing concerns about the transparency and fairness of AI systems, there's an increasing demand for AI ethics consulting. If you notice this trend early, you can invest in building expertise in AI ethics and offer consulting services to your clients, helping them ensure their AI systems are ethical and transparent.

**Pivoting and Adapting to Market Changes**

Being able to pivot and adapt to market changes is a crucial skill for any business, especially in a fast-changing field like AI and automation. Here's how you can do it:

**1. Flexible Business Model:** Design your business model to be flexible and adaptable. For instance, you can offer modular services that can be easily added, modified, or removed based on market demand.

**2. Rapid Prototyping:** If you have a new idea for a service or a solution, prototype it quickly and test it with a small set of clients. Based on the feedback, you can iterate and improve, or decide to pivot.

**3. Client-Centric Approach:** Always keep your clients at the center of your decision-making. Understand their changing needs and challenges, and adapt your services accordingly.

For instance, during the COVID-19 pandemic, many businesses had to shift to remote work. If your agency was offering automation solutions for office-based processes, you might have needed to pivot and start offering solutions for remote work processes.

## Staying Ahead in the AI Automation Industry

The AI automation industry is competitive, and staying ahead requires constant innovation, differentiation, and value delivery. Here are some strategies:

**1. Innovation:** Regularly invest in research and development to come up with new services, solutions, and approaches. This can help you stay ahead of your competitors and offer unique value to your clients.

**2. Differentiation:** Differentiate your agency by specializing in a niche, offering superior customer service, or building a strong brand. This can make your agency stand out and attract more clients.

**3. Value Delivery:** Continuously focus on delivering value to your clients. Understand their goals and challenges, and ensure your services and solutions are aligned with them.

For example, let's say you notice a trend where small businesses are struggling to leverage AI due to lack of expertise. To capitalize on this trend and stay ahead in the industry, you could develop a specialized offering for small businesses, providing them with simple, affordable, and customized AI automation solutions.

The world of AI and automation is full of opportunities for those who are prepared to navigate its trends, adapt to changes, and stay ahead in the industry. By adopting the strategies discussed in this chapter, your agency will not just survive but thrive in the future of AI automation.

## Chapter 12: Conclusion

As we reach the end of this comprehensive guide, it's time to consolidate our learning and take the next steps towards building a successful AI automation agency. In this final chapter, we will summarize the key takeaways from the book and outline actionable steps you can take to kickstart your journey to AI automation success.

**Key Takeaways**

**1. The Importance of AI and Automation:** AI and automation are transforming the business world, creating efficiencies and opportunities like never before. Starting an AI automation agency not only capitalizes on this trend but also enables you to contribute to this technological revolution.

**2. The Power of Zapier:** Zapier is a robust and versatile tool that can automate a wide range of business processes. As you've seen in our use cases, from automating email responses to streamlining project management, the possibilities are truly vast.

**3. Necessity of Market Research and Business Planning:** Understanding the AI automation landscape, identifying your niche, and crafting a solid business plan are crucial first steps to starting your agency.

**4. Agency Setup:** Starting an AI automation agency involves considering legal structure, assembling a capable team, and ensuring you have the right setup and equipment.

**5. Client-Centric Approach:** From identifying client needs to building and testing solutions, always keeping the client at the center ensures you deliver solutions that truly add value to their business.

**6. Marketing, Sales, and Project Management:** Effective branding, strategic marketing, persuasive sales techniques, and efficient project management are all critical for the success of your agency.

**7. Scaling and Future Trends:** Scaling your agency involves careful planning, effective talent management, and building systems for scale. Staying abreast of future trends in AI and automation ensures your agency remains relevant and competitive.

## Your Next Steps to AI Automation Success

With these key takeaways in mind, let's outline the next steps you should take to start your AI automation agency.

**1. Start Learning Zapier:** If you haven't already, start familiarizing yourself with Zapier. Try creating some simple 'Zaps' first, then experiment with more complex automation. Use the case studies we discussed as inspiration.

**2. Market Research:** Start researching your local market, identify potential clients and their needs.

Look for industries or businesses that could benefit significantly from AI automation.

**3. Business Plan:** Based on your market research, start crafting your business plan. Identify your unique selling proposition, determine your pricing structure, and set clear, measurable goals.

**4. Build Your Team:** Identify the skills and expertise you'll need in your team. Start recruiting or training your team members.

**5. Marketing and Sales:** Design your brand and start marketing your agency. Develop a website, start networking, and use both online and offline marketing strategies to attract your first clients.

**6. Continued Learning and Adaptation:** Finally, remember that starting your agency is just the beginning. Stay committed to continuous learning, be open to feedback, and always be ready to adapt.

To illustrate, let's imagine a hypothetical scenario: John, an IT professional, wants to start an AI automation agency. He starts by learning Zapier, experimenting with different 'Zaps'. He then researches local small businesses, identifying a need for automating marketing tasks. Using this information, he creates a business plan for an AI automation agency specializing in marketing automation for small businesses. He recruits a team of fellow IT professionals and starts marketing his agency, using the strategies discussed in this book. With determination and continuous learning, John gradually builds a successful AI automation agency.

As you embark on your journey, remember that the road to success is rarely straight or smooth.

There will be challenges, but with the right mindset, the right tools, and the right strategies, you can overcome them and build a successful AI automation agency. It's an exciting journey ahead, and we wish you the very best. Your AI automation success story starts now.

9 798215 514856